SALESMAN'S LITTLE BOOK OF WISDOM

Written by Scott E. Power
Edited by Chuck Kostell

ICS BOOKS, Inc.
Merrillville. IN

Salesman's Little Book of Wisdom
Copyright © 1997 by Scott Power
10 9 8 7 6 5 4 3 2 1
All inquiries should be addressed to ICS Books, Inc., 1370 E. 86th Place, Merrillville, IN 46410

Published by:	**Co-Published in Canada by;**	**Printed in the U.S.A.**
ICS BOOKS, Inc.	Vanwell Publishing LTD	
1370 E. 86th Place	1 Northrup Crescent	
Merrillville, IN 46410	St. Catharines, Ontario	Cover Photos: PhotoDisc
800-541-7323	L2M 6P5	
	800-661-6136	

Library of Congress Cataloging-in-Publication Data

Power, Scott E..
    Salesman's little book of wisdom / by Scott Power.
    p.   cm. -- (Little books of wisdom series)
    ISBN 1-57034-061-7 (pb)
1. Selling--Quotations, maxims, etc.
               I. Title. II Series .
               HF5438.25.P69 1997
               658.8'5--dc21
                                  96-29839
                                    CIP

Dedication:

This book is dedicated to Chuck Kostell,
a dear friend, mentor, and one of the
world's greatest salesman.

Introduction

There are few job opportunities out there with as much promise for economic gain as sales. "You can make so much money!" is the promise we hear as the proverbial carrot is waved in front of our nose. Yes, we can make a lot of money but, the realization of this fantasy is often preceded by months of hard work, dead-end leads, and frustration before we ever see a profit. Often times, the faint-hearted give up in haste disgusted wondering why they didn't make their fortune as promised. What happened? After all, they listened to motivational audio tapes, read all of Zig Ziglar's books, quoted daily affirmations, and even followed the advice of all those successful senior-level executives who drive sports cars and live on the lake. Well, according to my observations, there are two key reasons why people succeed in accomplishing their expectations for sales, and even life in general: realistic goals and perseverance.

1. Remember Secretary's Day.

2. Remember your secretary's birthday.

3. Remember your client's birthday.

4.   When out making sales calls remember to call in for messages.

5.   Compliment your fellow employees and support staff.

6.   Customer service will get you the sale before price point will.

7. Set one, three, six, and ten month goals for yourself.

8. The essence of any business is sales.

9. Don't be greedy. It's a great way to lose a client.

10. Salesmen don't sell products or services. Salesmen sell solutions.

11. Customer service is paramount.

12. Make your client feel he's the most important one you've got.

13. Your client is the key to your success. If you don't take care of him, someone else will.

14. Save your receipts. Your business related purchases are tax deductible.

15. Save your client's time and money and you'll have sales.

16. When beginning a new sales position, expect six months of hard work before you see substantial results.

17. Plan your work, work your plan.

18. You must take a risk to achieve success.

19. Believe strongly if your product or service.

20. Often, price is more of a problem in the sales person's mind than the customer.

21. Many customers start out price-conscious, but end up becoming value-conscious.

22. Price + quality + service = VALUE.

23. When a product or service is complex or personalized, the price becomes less important.

24.   Generally, when the price is high, extra
       benefits and "intangible" values must
       be sold.

25.   Learn to act, not react.

26.   In business, reinvest a portion of all you
       make, keep a portion for your use, save
       a portion for those in need.

27. Consider your appearance an outward expression of your inward commitment to excellence.

28. Great works are performed not by strength, but by perseverance.
-Samuel Johnson

29.   It's the constant and determined effort that breaks down all resistance, sweeps away all obstacles.

- Claude M. Bristol

30.   I think the person who takes a job in order to live--that is to say, (just) for the money-has turned himself into a slave.

- Joseph Campbell

31.　Never before have the latest and best marketing and sales practices been more essential in conquering new markets and defending hard won gains.

32.　Do not keep clients waiting for you if possible. Take messages and call people back, rather than keeping them on hold. The customer standing in front of you is priority at the moment. They came to see you.

33.   Very important: Call clients back as soon as possible. Even if you don't have an answer, call with an update.

34.   Strength and justice are the products of a steady heart.

- Zen proverb.

35.   No matter how difficult the past, you can always begin again today.

36. Happiness comes when your work and words are of benefit to yourself and others.

37. Do not be afraid to say, "I don't know," but be prompt in getting the answer to your customer and they will be happy that you made the effort.

38. Sales is a art.

39. Selling is basically negotiating.

40. Black's Law Dictionary defines "Breach of Contract" as, "failure, without legal excuse, to perform any promise which forms the whole or part of a contract."

41. Don't worry about wealth.

42. If you do your job right, wealth will follow.

43. There are five elements of the effective sales call: preparation, structure, styles, and follow-up.

44. People will buy on principle.

45. Price is not always the bottom line.

46. If you give good service and make a positive impression, customers will come back or give you first chance with an order, before going to a competitor.

47. Man has just two inborn passions: to get and to get.

48. We all role play in life. A good salesman masters this skill.

49.   Know your merchandise.

50.   Know your competitor's merchandise.

51.   Shut one eye and you can't hear
      everything. Watch you client's body
      language.

52.   People are governed by the head; a kind
      heart is of little value in sales.

53.   Every luxury must be paid for, and
      everything is a luxury, starting with
      being in the world.

      - Pavese

54.   Sales is not a spectacle or a feast; it is a
      predicament.

55.   Simply the thing you sell shall make
      you live.

56. Work for a living. Play for a life.

57. Never let work get in the way of your career.

58. Life is too short not to sell.

59. Whenever you have a significant conversation with an account, in person or by phone, write a call report and put in the account's folder.

60. We're all blind just dreaming we can see.

61. The iron chain and the golden handcuffs are both equally bonds.

62. The basic test of freedom is perhaps less in what we are free to sell than in what we are free not to sell.

63.   Know your competition.

64.   Know your prospect's competition.

65.   A salesperson's worst difficulties begin
        when he is able to do as he likes.

66.   A good management team provides
        focus.

67.   The eyes are more exact witnesses than the ears.

- Heraclitus

68.   Action speak louder than words.

69.   Sales speak louder than words.

70.   There is an essential ambiguity in human gestures, and when someone raises the palms of his hands together, we do not know whether it is to bury himself in prayer or to throw himself into the sea.

- Ortega Y Gasset

71.   The idealist walks on tiptoe, the materialist on his heels, the salesman on the pavement.

72. Anger is never without an argument, but
     seldom with a good one.
                                    - Halifax

73. Hacks care what happens to others only
     in proportion as it affects sales, but
     good salespeople bring humanity to
     work with them.

74. Maintain an account folder on each of your accounts containing important dates, names, call reports, sales letters, follow-up letters, other materials pertinent to the account.

75. Believe in what you do and in what you sell or move on.

76. Find something to sell that you like. It will be easier to talk about and you'll be more convincing.

77. The tragedy of sales is not so much what salesmen suffer, but rather what sales they miss.

78. Review your files regularly and always refer to them in planning your sales calls.

79. Extreme behavior is rarely productive or healthy.

80. We are never as successful or unsuccessful as we think we are.

81. If we only wanted to be rich it would be easy; but we want to be richer than other people, which is almost always difficult, since we think them richer than they are.

82. Cover yourself always in writing. All of it. Shipping date, costs, any special deals, etc. If not, it will come back to haunt you sooner or later.

83. Only a poor salesman sold more of his time that he has too.

84. It is an aspect of all success to suppose that we deserve it.

85. When you have an appointment in one particular part of your territory, make additional appointments nearby at suitable times. This way you cover all of your territory thoroughly.

86. Never put off until tomorrow what can be done today.

87. Success is found in the details.

88.   One's real life is often the life that one does not lead.

   - Wilde

89.   Make appointments one and two weeks in advance and be thinking about what appointments you are going to make for the third week.

90.   It is impossible for a man to be cheated
      by anyone but himself.
                                  - Emerson

91.   Nothing is impossible.

92.   We have to prove ourselves many years
      before we gain our own confidence.

93.   If you need any help in organization, in settling up forms and files, in strategy, letter writing, call on your management. That's what they're there for.

94.   Not all those who know their markets know their hearts as well.

95. Our greatest pretenses are built up not to hide our failure and the ugly in us, but our emptiness. The hardest thing to hide is something that is not there.

96. Avoid the over-use of "you" in a sales letter as it becomes excessive.

97. Absurdity of conduct comes from trying to be something your not.

98. Never say 'no' to a customer unless you know that you cannot give them what they need or want.

99. If you know someone else who can help them, tell them. Many grateful customers will come back because of your honesty.

100. It pays off on a bigger scale in the end to put the client's needs first, before the dollar.

101. Dreams influence actions.

102. Money and debt are responsible for all our actions; money causes our voluntary acts, debt our involuntary.

103. Passion makes man sell, his wisdom makes him succeed.

104. One poor deal is never cured by another.

105. We are sometimes moved by greed and suppose it's passion.

106. Fanaticism consists in redoubling your effort when you have forgotten your aim.

    - Santayana

107. It is unhealthy to suppress your true feelings. Always be honest about the way you feel.

108. No indulgence of passion destroys the spiritual nature so much as respectable selfishness.

    -MacDonald

109. Sell with confidence and people will buy.

110. He who desires but acts not, breeds pestilence.

    - Blake

111. You cannot win them all, just try.

112. "Every man has his price." This is not true. But for every man there exists a bait which he cannot resist swallowing. To win over certain people to something, it is only necessary to give it a gloss of love of humanity, nobility, gentleness, self-sacrifice - and there is nothing you cannot get them to swallow.

    - Nietzsche

113. You sell therefore you live.

114. Study how other salesmen become successful.

115. Joy in being right comes from proving others wrong.

116. When a man say him do not mind, then him mind.

- African Proverb

117.   No one lies so boldly as the man who is indignant.

- Nietzsche

118.   It is hard to believe that a man is telling the truth when you know that you would lie if you were in his place.

- Mencken

119.   Honesty is often in the wrong.

- Lucan

120. Honesty is the best policy.

121. Generally, your first reaction is the wrong one. Wait a bit to think, then react.

122. Salesmen not very strong in memory should not lie.

123. The successful man will profit from his mistakes and try again in a different way.

-Dale Carnage

124. The fox condemns the trap, not himself.

- Blake

125. The greatest of faults, I should say, is to be conscious of none.

- Dr. Johnson

126. The most powerful types of sales letters are birthday or anniversary greetings, thank you notes or business congratulations.

127. Almost all our faults are more forgivable than the methods we resort to hide them.

    - La Rochefoucauld

128. Consult management before quoting
     alternatives to company policy.
     Promises made in haste can cause big
     problems and bad feelings with clients.

129. Whatever you condemn, you have done
     yourself.

     - Groddeck

130. How glorious it is - and also how painful - to be an exception.

   - Musset

131. Nothing moves unless someone sells it.

132. There is an luxury in self-reproach. When we blame ourselves we feel no one else has a right to blame us.

   - Wilde

133. You can't learn anything when you are talking. Stop and listen to the customer.

134. The sale begins when the customer says 'no.'

135. All salesmen hate rejection. Good salesmen learn from it.

136. Customers may retain 10% of what you tell him. A follow up letter reviewing your main points makes the sale easier.

137. Don't promise what you know you can't deliver, everyone loses.

138. Vanity plays lurid tricks with our memory.

- Conrad.

139. Always ask for the order. Don't be afraid of rejection.

140. Always mistrust a subordinate who never finds fault with his superior.
     - *Collins*

141. It is better to speak wisdom foolishly, like the saints, rather than to speak folly wisely, like the dons.
     - *Chesterton*

142. Preparation is more important than the sales presentation itself.

143. Never knock the competition unless you want the customer to think about them.

144. Patience is a most necessary quality for business.

145. When a merchant speaks of sheep he means the hide.
     - *Swiss Proverb*

146. The by-product is sometimes more valuable than the product.
     - *Ellis*

147. A corporation cannot blush. It's integrity must always be protected.

148. Do not underestimate "word-of-mouth" influences, good or bad.

149. Men of business must not break their word twice.
- Thomas Fuller

150. Whatever is not nailed down is mine. Whatever I can pry loose is not nailed down.
- Ascribed to Collis P. Huntington

151. To be successful teach your aspirations to confirm themselves to fact, not the other way around.

152. Clever liars give details, but the cleverest don't.

153. A salesman who lies is disregarded by customers and worthless to his company.

154. If you want to know what a man is really like, take notice how he acts when he loses money.
    - *New England Proverb*

155. As a general rule, nobody has money who ought to have it.
    - *Disraeli*

156. A wise man knows everything; a shrewd one, everybody.

157. Distrust anyone who likes you extremely upon just meeting you.

158. He who praises you for what you lack wishes to take from you what you have.
   - *Juan Manuel*

159. There is a division of labor, even in vice. Some people addict themselves to the speculation only, others to the practice.

   - *Hazlitt*

160. Talk about the customer's business and relate your product or service to it.

161. Always follow-up with clients. Always.

162. Don't overwhelm the customer with complex statistics from research. Be selective and relate it to the customer's problems or needs.

163. He that fears you present will hate you absent.

    - Thomas Fuller

164. The consequences of anger are often far greater than the causes of it.

165. Workaholics eventually burn out. Take time to relax on vacations and weekends, so you start the work week refreshed.

166. Strive to be superior to yourself rather than your equals.

167. Salesmen are very apt to complain of the ingratitude of those who have risen far above him.

168. Familiarity in one's superiors causes bitterness, for it may not be returned.
      - Nietzsche

169. Socialize with those who inspire and motivate you instead of those who discourage you.

170. Confronted by outstanding merit in another, there is no way of saving one's ego except by love.

     - Goethe

171. The salesman who can't sell says the market is down.

172. There are many sales that we would pass up, if we were not afraid that some one else would get them.

173. We grow tired of everything but ridiculing others and congratulating ourselves.

174. Cheating in any form is the personification of inability.

175. You can't sell sitting on you butt. Go out and meet the customer face to face.

176. A lazy person always knows the time.

177. To be idle and to be poor have always been reproaches, and therefore every man endeavors with his utmost care to hide his poverty from others, and his idleness from himself.

    - Dr. Johnson

178. Never put off until tomorrow what can be ignored altogether.

179. Develop a selling vocabulary of words that are specific and leave no room for ambiguity.

180. Work with some men is as besetting a sin as idleness with others.
     - Samuel Butler (II)

181. Not everything that is more difficult is more meritorious.

       - Saint Thomas Aquinas

182. The customer is always right. Go back and do your homework.

183. Sometimes, less is more. Tell customers what they need to know and don't confuse them with too many details unless they ask.

184. Never pass up the opportunity to thank the customer for his business.

185. A good salesman can put himself in the place of a bad one more easily than a bad salesman can put himself in the place of a good one.

186. One good sale has many claimants.

187. A little money saved early in life can help you retire as a millionaire. It's called compounding. Figure it out.

188. Real unselfishness consists in helping others.

189. Never let your career get in the way of your family.

190. Never let your career get in the way of your family.

191. While it's important to know everyone in a particular department, be sure your primary sales effort is directed at the decision maker.

192. Don't waste the prospect's time with useless conversation about sports trivia or your children's accomplishments. His time is valuable get to the point of business.

193. A visitor to New York City asked a street musician how one gets to Carnegie Hall. After a brief moment, the musician replied, "Practice, practice, practice!"

194. First impressions are critical, so you must practice your presentations over and over until they become effective.

195. A wise salesman sells as much as necessary, not as much as he can.

196. Wisdom consists in knowing how far to go when going too far.

197.   Tact is the intelligence of the heart.

198.   Put first things first. Rank these tasks by importance, not difficulty.

199.   Ambitious salesmen have as much energy as they need to surpass their sales projections.

200. Ambition is pitiless. Any merit that it cannot use it finds despicable.

- Jobber

201. Nothing is enough to the man for whom enough is too little.

- Epicurus

202. A successful salesman never thinks that his job is boring.

203. Everybody wants to be somebody: nobody wants to grow.

> *- Goethe*

204. Salesmen who succeed in meeting their goals are those who possess good digestive systems.

205. To close a sale, to promote action, you must reach the people who make buying decisions.

206. Every salesman who refuses to accept the conditions of life works harder than those who don't.

207. I must complain the cards are ill-shuffled, till I have a good hand.
       - *Swift*

208. A prudent man will appreciate what he has versus what he doesn't .

209. Make sure your prospective customer understands what you are selling.

210. A good salesman will make more opportunities than he finds.

211. To maintain that our successes are due to Providence and not to our own cleverness is a cunning way of increasing in our own eyes the importance of our successes.

-Pavese

212. Fortune does not change men; it unmasks them.
   - *Mme. Necker*

213. Adversity introduces a man to himself.

214. Experience is only half of experience.
   - *Goethe*

215. Experience is not what happens to a salesman. It is what a salesmen does with what happens to him.

216. Few salesmen are worthy of experience. The majority let it corrupt them.

217. Experience is the name everyone gives to his mistakes.

- Wilde

218.   Work hard to eliminate misconceptions about the product or service you are selling.

219.   Many are stubborn in pursuit of the path they have chosen, few in pursuit of the goal.

-Nietzsche

220. Hope is generally a wrong guide,
     though it is very good company along
     the way.

     - Halifax

221. Every year, if not every day, we have to
     wager our salvation upon some
     prophecy based upon imperfect
     knowledge.

     - O.W. Holmes, Jr.

222. Hope is good in the morning, but bad at bedtime.

223. Ask your prospects how they buy and what they buy, so you can focus your presentation.

224. The basis of optimism is sheer terror.
    - *Wilde*

225. A pessimist salesman is one who has been compelled to work with a successful one.

226. Salesmen succeed in enterprises which demand the positive qualities they possess, but they excel in those which can also make use of their defects.

227. A salesman should not bother to eliminate his complexes, but to get into accord with them.

228. To do great work a salesman must be very patient as well as very industrious.

229. Talent without genius isn't much, but genius without talent is nothing whatever.

- Valery

230. To measure up to all that is demanded of him, a salesman must overestimate himself.

231. Consciousness of our powers empowers us.

232. Nature reacts not only to physical disease, but also to moral weakness; when the danger increases, she gives us greater courage only if we are courageous enough to take it.

233. A salesman who continues to fail in his pursuit of wealth and power will eventually give in to lying and cheating.

234. The greatest mistake any salesman can make is to continually think he will make one.

235. A wise salesman finds he has been wrong at every preceding stage of his career, only to deduce the astonishing conclusion that he succeeded anyway.

236. It is often the successful one who pioneers new lands, new undertakings, new forms of expression, making the way for those who come after.

237. The secret of success is known only to those who have failed.

238. Even Rockefeller and Ford had to start by working hard.

239. Prospects often reveal their preferences in off hand remarks.

240. Help your prospects develop clear-cut objectives by helping them understand what their options are.

241. Success causes stress. Have regular check-ups with your physician.

242. Everyone has a need to be conceited until successful.

243. The common idea that success spoils people by making them vain, egotistic, and self-complacent is erroneous; on the contrary, it makes them, for the most part, humble, tolerant, and kind. Failure makes people cruel and bitter.
- *Maugham*

244. Money is the fools priest and the wise man's servant.

245. Salesmen, be romantic about love, but not about money.

246. Money, it turned out, was exactly like sex; you thought of nothing else if you didn't have it and thought of other things if you did.

- James Baldwin

247. If women didn't exist, all the money in the world would have no meaning.
    - Aristotle Onassis

248. Make money and the whole world will conspire to call you a gentleman.
    - Mark Twain

249. So you think that money is the root of all evil. Have you ever asked what is the root of money?
    -Ayn Rand

250. The love of money is the root of all evil, not money itself.

251. The petty economics of the rich are just as amazing as the silly extravagances of the poor.

- William Feather

252. Money is a terrible master, but an excellent servant.

- P.T. Barnum

253.   Suggest alternatives to customers if you
       do not have exactly what they want.

254.   Money may be the husk of many things,
       but not the kernel. It brings you food,
       but not appetite; medicine, but not
       health, acquaintances, but not friends;
       servants, but not faithfulness; days of
       joy, but not peace or happiness.
                                   -Henrik Ibsen

255. The entire essence of America is the hope to first make money-then make money with money- then make lots of money with lots of money.
    - Paul Erdman

256. The highest use of capital is not to make money, but to make money do more for the betterment of life.
    - Henry Ford

257.   The more money an American
         accumulates, the less interesting he
         becomes.

                                    - Gore Vidal

258.   Finance is the art of passing currency
         from hand to hand until it finally
         disappears.

                                 - Robert Sarnoff

259. Finance is the art or science of managing revenues and resources for the best advantage of the manager.
    - *Ambrose Bierce*

260. Where large sums of money are concerned, it is advisable to trust nobody.
    - *Agatha Christie*

261. Surplus wealth is a sacred trust which its possessor is bound to administer in his lifetime for the good of the community.

   - Andrew Carnegie

262. Prosperity is only an instrument to be used, not a deity to be worshiped.

   - Calvin Coolidge

263. Make money your God, and your life will be hell.

264. Nothing is wrong with men possessing riches, but its wrong when riches possess men.

265. Promise to be sincere, not impartial.

266. The universal appeal in effective clear-cut objectives helps salesmen understand what their options are.

267. Being poor is a state of mind. Being broke is a temporary situation.

268. I have tried to become conservative. In 1958, I resolved to be simply a piano player. That was the year I lost $800,000.

- Liberace

269. A good sales letter puts the spotlight on the customer or prospect.

270. The trouble with being poor is that it takes up all your time.
    - William De Kooning

271. Poverty is uncomfortable; but nine times out of ten the best thing that can happen to a young man is to be tossed overboard and compelled to sink or swim.
    - James A. Garfield

272. Almost all the noblest things that have been achieved in the world have been achieved by poor men, poor scholars, poor professional men, poets and men of genius. A certain steadiness and sobriety, a certain moderation and restraint, a certain pressure of circumstances are good for men. His body was not made for luxuries. It sickens, sinks and dies under them.

- Henry David Thoreau

273. I'd like to live like a poor man with lots of money.

      - Pablo Picasso

274. I never wanted to be a millionaire. I just wanted to live like one.

      - Walter Hagen

275. Most people seek after what they do not possess and are enslaved by the very things they want to acquire.

      - Anwar El-Sadat

276. In God we trust, all others pay cash.
-Sign used in retail stores during the Depression.

277. It is better to give that to lend, and it costs about the same.
- Sir Philip Gibbs

278. Credit buying is much like being drunk. The buzz happens immediately and gives you a lift...The hangover comes the day after.

    - Dr. Joyce Brothers

279. A penny saved is a penny earned. Economy is a source of great revenue.

280. Be sure that you put the client's product or company name into your sales letters.

281. Avoid two or three page sales letter.

282. There are only two times in a man's life
      when he should not speculate; when he
      can't afford it, and when he can.
      - Mark Twain

283. You can always put multiple points into
      a presentation folder.

284. The bulls make money. The bears make
      money. But the pigs get slaughtered.
      - Wall Street axiom

285. Begin your sales letter with something
      the customer or prospect has said to
      you. People love to read their own
      words.

286. We have a love-hate relationship. We hate inflation, but we love everything that causes it.
      -William Simon

287. A nickel ain't worth a dime anymore.
      - Yogi Berra

287. The best thing that can come with success is the knowledge that it is nothing to long for.
      - Liv Ullman

288. Success has always been the greatest liar.

290. It is not enough to succeed. Others must fail.
     - Gore Vidal

291. The most successful salesman holds onto the old just as long as it's new, and grabs the new just as soon as it better.

292. Successful people are the ones who can think up stuff for the rest of the world to keep busy at.

    - Don Marquis

293. The toughest thing about success is that you've got to keep it up.

294. Every successful enterprise requires three men - a dreamer, a businessman, and a son-of-a-bitch.

    - Peter McCarthur

295.   The secret of Japanese success is not technology, but a special way of managing people - style that focuses a strong company philosophy, a distinct corporate culture, long-range staff development, and consensus decision-making.

- William Ouchi

296. A persuasive sales presentation is based on structure and organization that addresses your prospects special needs.

297. A presentation of 8 to 10 minutes should be long enough to say what you need to say.

298. Always be polite, even in uncomfortable situations. People do lose their tempers from time to time and two wrongs don't make a right.

299. A banker is a fellow who lends you his umbrella when the sun is shining and wants it back the minute it begins to rain.

-Mark Twain

300. If you wish it, do it.

301. Basic, good salesmanship starts with a compassionate attitude regarding your clients.

302. The banks couldn't afford me. That's why I had to be in business for myself.
      - Samuel Goldwyn

303. It's American to start one's own business.

    - Anne McDonnell Ford

304. Befriending someone is the easiest thing is the world, just be nice. It is easier to sell to a friend than a stranger.

305. The real problem is what to do with the problem solvers after the problems are solved.

    - Gay Talese

306. The ability to deal with people is as purchasable a commodity as sugars or coffee. And I pay more for that ability than for any other under the sun.

   - John D. Rockefeller, Jr.

307. The greatest ability in business is to get along with others and influence their actions. A chip on the shoulder is too heavy a piece of baggage to carry through life.

   - John Hancock

308. When two men in business always
       agree, one of them is unnecessary.
                    - *William Wrigley, Jr.*

309. A good salesperson knows how to
       effectively manage a territory and/or
       assigned accounts. Effective selling is
       organized selling.

310. Organize your materials so that you can use them productively.

311. Your reputation is everything in business.

312. An oral contract isn't worth the paper it's written on.

   - Samual Goldwyn

313. Establish specific objectives for your sales calls and then communicate them to your customer. The more specific the objective, the better the opportunity to close the sale.

314. Selling requires active listening.

315. Man matures through work which inspires him to difficult good.
- Pope John Paul II

316. Don't talk about how hard you work. Show how much you get done.

317. When your work speaks for itself, don't interrupt.
   - *Henry Kaiser*

318. A man's work is a portrait of himself.

319. Work smart then, work hard.

320. If he works for you, you work for him.
   - *Japanese Proverb*

321. It is not the employer who pays wages -
he only handles the money. It is the
product that pays wages.
- Henry Ford

322. There are two things needed in these
days; first, for rich men to find out how
poor men live; and, second, for poor
men to know how rich men work.
- E. Atkinson

323. It is easier to do a job right than to explain why you didn't.
      - Martin Van Buren

324. The salesperson who sells creatively doesn't have to sell competitively.

325. In a hierarchy, every employee tends to rise to his superior's level of incompetence.

326. If A equals success, then the formula is A equals X plus Y, with X being work, Y play, and Z keeping your mouth shut.
    - Albert Einstein

327. Learn to be good at handling objections, stalls, and complaints.

328. The world is full of willing people; some willing to work, the rest willing to let them.

    - Robert Frost

329. It never fails; salesmen who really succeed do it by busting their ass.

330. Anticipate questions and problems and be prepared with answers.

331. There is more to life than increasing its speed.

- Mahatma Gandhi

332. Opportunities are usually disguised as hard work, so most people don't recognize them.
    - *Ann Landers*

333. Small opportunities are often the beginning of great enterprise.
    - *Demosthenes*

334. Luck means the hardships and privations which you have not hesitated to endure, the long nights you have devoted to work. Luck means the appointments you have never failed to keep; the trains you have never failed to catch.

- Max O'Rell

335. Progress in industry depends very largely on the enterprise of open-minded men who can think for themselves.

336. Your customer's concerns and life effect the business relationship you have with them.

337.   The man who will use his skill and
        constructive imagination to see how
        much he can give for a dollar, instead of
        how little he can give for a dollar, is
        bound to succeed.
                                    - Henry Ford

338.   If you want to succeed you should
        strike out on new paths rather than
        travel the worn paths of accepted
        success.
                            - John D. Rockefeller, Jr.

339. Punctuality is the soul of business.
     -Thomas Haliburton

340. Time is money.

341. The reason why worry kills more
     people than work is that more people
     worry than work. -
     -Robert Frost

342. If you aren't fired with enthusiasm, you'll be fired with enthusiasm.
     - *Vince Lombardi*

343. By the time you get to the close of a sale, you should simply be confirming agreements you and your prospect have already reached.

344. Don't be misled into believing that somehow the world owes you a living. The boy who believes that his parents, or the government, or anyone else owes him his livelihood and that he can collect it without labor will wake up one day and find himself working for another boy who did not have that belief and, therefore, earned the right to have others work for him.

-David Sarnoff

345. The brain is a wonderful organ; it starts working the moment you get up in the morning and doesn't stop until you get into the office.

    - Robert Frost

346. Desktop presentation computer software enables salespeople to created dynamic presentation materials - slides, transparencies, hand outs - all in house.

347. Salesmen can do jointly what they cannot do singly; and the union of minds and hands, the concentration of their power, becomes almost omnipotent.

348. It's a recession when your neighbor loses his job; it's a depression when you lose yours.

   - Harry Truman

349. Being a woman is a terribly difficult task, since it consists principally in dealing with men.

    -Joseph Conrad

350. Computer presentation software saves time and money by letting you do-it-yourself.

351. The business of government is to keep the government out of business-that is, unless business needs government aid.
   -Will Rogers

352. In business, the competition will bite you if you keep running; if you stand still, they will swallow you.
   - Leo Cherne

353. Consider time elements when scheduling appointments, give yourself plenty of time for meetings and travel.

354. Think of the future when you sell. What will the client need six months from now?

355.   An advantage in desktop presentation software is its extensive selection of professionally designed templates with borders, bullets, colors, font style and sizes that help make a dynamic presentation.

356.   Everything comes to him who hustles while he waits.

- Thomas Alva Edison

357. The average person puts only 25% of his energy and ability into his work. The world takes off its hat to those who put in more than 50% of their capacity, and stands on its head for those few and far between who devote 100%.

- Andrew Carnegie

358. Work expands so as to fill the time available for its completion.
     - C. Northcote Parkinson

359. Don't bother about genius. Don't worry about being clever. Trust to hard work, perseverance and determination. And the best motto for the long march is: "Don't grumble. Plug on!"
     -Sir Frederick Treves

360. Most of life is routine-dull and grubby, but routine is the momentum that keeps a man going. If you wait for inspiration you'll be standing on the corner after the parade is a mile down the street.
- *Ben Nicholas*

361. Concentration is my motto-first honesty, then industry, then concentration.
-Andrew Carnegie

362.   Until you understand Capitalism you do
       not understand human society as it
       exists at present.
                            -George Bernard Shaw

363.   Smartly crafted flip charts,
       transparencies, and other presentation
       materials now can be done in minutes
       with computer software such as
       Microsoft PowerPoint and Aldus
       Persuasion.

364. The craft of the merchant is this,
     bringing a thing from where it abounds
     to where it is costly.
                        -Ralph Waldo Emerson

365. It is well-known what a middleman is:
     he is a man who bamboozles one party
     and plunders the other.
                        -Benjamin Disraeli

366. Commerce via the Internet will eventually create a new class of middlemen.

367. Sales is the art of commerce.

368. Make three correct guesses consecutively and you will establish a reputation as an expert.
    -Laurence Peter

369. The successful businessman sometimes makes his money by ability and experience, but he generally makes it by mistake.

- G.K. Chesterton

370. Be awful nice to 'em goin' up, because you're going to meet 'em comin' down.

- Jimmy Durante

371.   Hitch your wagon to a star.
          -Ralph Waldo Emerson

372.   The best executive is the one who has
         sense enough to pick good men to do
         what he wants done, and self-restraint
         enough to keep from meddling with
         them while they do it.
                   - Theodore Roosevelt.

373. Nothing is quite honest that is not commercial, but not everything commercial is honest.
    -Robert Frost

374. Sales in the oldest of the arts, the newest of professions.

375. Salesmen must not break their word.

376.   Nothing is illegal if a hundred businessmen decide to do it, and that's true anywhere in the world.

   - Andrew Young

377.   Whatever may be the case in the court of morals, there is no legal obligation on the vendor to inform the purchaser that his is under a mistake, not induced by the act of the vendor.

   - Justice Blackburn

378. The secret in business is to know
     something that nobody else knows.
     - Aristotle Onassis

379. Too many executives tend to follow the
     road proved safe, rather than the
     dynamic approach of self-reliance,
     individualism and initiative.
     - Louis E. Wolfson

380. Corporate American does not hire natural-born leaders. They hire followers, people of average intelligence, who are reliable and will do the job without asking why or rocking the boat. This is the curse of all leaders; they must find their own way.

381. Business has only two basic functions - innovation and sales.

382. A man is known by the company he organizes.

-Ambrose Bierce

383. Try not to become a man of success but rather try to become a man of value.

- Albert Einstein

384. Start your sales presentation with an overview of the topic, then explain the main points, and conclude by delving into the specifics.

385. Always challenge popular opinion. Be a skeptic.

386. Build integrity before wealth.

387. Remember to be courteous.

388. Be a student of life.

389. If your afraid of commitment, others will be afraid of you.

390. There is more to life than money.

391. Always try to have printed materials to be handed out afterward that recap your presentation. Tell the audience ahead of time so they won't feel they should take notes.

392. Have a one, three, five, ten, and twelve year marketing plan for your life. This way you will see where you want to go and the best way to get there.

393. Work to express yourself.

394. No one sales is ever going to be important to you. No one sale is going to tell you who you are or who you will be.

395. Selling is easy if you work hard enough.

396. Achievement is not synonymous with competition.

397. Think strategically.

398. Always be accountable to your clients.

399. Service is an attitude, not a department.

400. Empower yourself.

401. Read everything you can. Knowledge is power.

402. Have a sales mentor.

403. Before responding to any objection, get more information to help you understand why.

404.   Sales is the art of commerce.

405.   Commerce is the art of economy.

406.   Economy is the art of life.

407.   Life is the art of existence.